I0421462

Francesca Salierno

BENEATH THE FILTERS

The Dangerous Effects of Social Media on Mental Health

AUSTIN MACAULEY PUBLISHERS™

LONDON • CAMBRIDGE • NEW YORK • SHARJAH

A CIP catalogue record for this title is available from the British Library.

ISBN 9781035832262 (Paperback)
ISBN 9781035832255 (ePub e-book)

www.austinmacauley.com

First Published 2023
Austin Macauley Publishers Ltd®
1 Canada Square
Canary Wharf
London
E14 5AA

Chapter 1
Lose Weight

I'll start this chapter with words that should be abolished, erased from our vocabulary, eliminated, burned at the stake, tied to a boulder and dropped to the bottom of the deepest ocean. However, you will, completely destroyed and never to be again re-evoked by any woman on this planet: lose weight.

If you think I'm exaggerating, you don't know my story and that of most of the women that surround me. At 14 years of age, when my hormones shifted and initiated my transition to womanhood. I became the subject of insistent pressures, in the various environments in which I found myself (school, work, home) that were urging me to lose weight.

Nobody told me, at the start of my transition from child to woman, 'Darling, what a wonderful transformation you're now experiencing. This is the start of a magnificent new era. Listen, don't be afraid because your hormones are a mess, or about the fact that you want to consume the entire Nutella factory. You just have to learn to live with these new feelings and find a balance. You can do it! Whatever doesn't kill us makes us stronger.'

Rather, the dialogues were diverse yet all basically centred on the one dreaded message: "you must lose weight". Countless appointments with dieticians alternated with periods of uncontrolled eating causing a cycle of eating misery.

Never could I have imagined that anyone, specifically a woman, could exist without being on a diet. It was a concept that was, to me, completely alien. I would have had an easier time understanding string theory and quantum physics. My friends were all (and still are) on diets. My mother cooked healthy food all because my father and I were on a diet which of course meant she was too, for us. Only people on diets surrounded me, and I am certain that mine was not a unique experience.

Millions of people around the world are in search of the magic pill for weight loss. It's a billion-dollar industry. Dieticians prescribe diets that are stuck with for a day or two then abandoned. Authors write books on how to lose weight. Trainers, qualified or not, sell programs online, with promises of instant results. Deluding themselves, people start with hopes of success, only to stop and restart, creating an infinite and vicious circle, one that will hold a place as the protagonist in the lives of too many women. This is without mention of the eating disorders that are increasingly destroying the lives of our young adults and children. Remember there are no magic cures and if something seems to be too good to be true – it is.

Whatever the case may be, having been a veritable test subject for every diet ever created, I feel I at least have a right bring to light the results of experiments conducted on my body and more importantly my mind for years. I am enthusiastic to share the conclusions of my study. Despite the negative prognosis, I was, luckily, able to find psychological serenity, and in the end with it a *pretty good physique*, without ever uttering the word diet. Or for that matter going on a diet.

My revolution commenced in 2015. Exhausted by my extremely conflicted relationship with my body and my diet, I turned to a psychologist as a final attempt at help. I figured my mind had just as much to do with this as my body. After giving me such superb advice, such as concentration on your breathing and performance of cardiac coherence exercises on YouTube, she recommended *The Paradoxical Diet*, a book addressing the failure of diets, by an Italian author.

Desperate for answers, I ran home, downloaded the book, and devoured it in one sitting. It was at this point that I reached the end of my tether, the point of no return. The author, and consequently my psychotherapist, advised addressing the eating disorder by striving to eat ten times the amount of what is craved. Do you desire pizza or chocolate? Apply the rule of ten: force yourself to eat ten pizzas and ten chocolate bars of your choice. *I'll show you how the desire passes* – seemed to be the intended narrative of the author. In hindsight this was terrible advice but like they say hindsight is 20–20.

I went on a rampage, inside me a voice repeatedly incessantly, like an echo: 'THAT'S ENOUGH. THIS IS CRAZY!'

I vowed I would never, in my life, ever diet again. Tired of the judgment and commands from people who had evidently never been a woman in the grip of an eating disorder, I understood that the only way to escape was to come up with a new, more realistic and above all, feasible method.

The first thing I felt after having made this decision was extreme uneasiness. After all, I was going against pretty much everything everybody told me up until this day. Part of me was thinking: could everybody really be wrong? Bitter thoughts of being doomed to remain in these physical and mental states for the rest of my life plagued me. At the same time, I felt somewhat heartened by the idea of never again being at the mercy of the world of dieting.

Certainly, though, I couldn't deny the physiological aspects and causes of the fall back into self-destructive thoughts. At times I found myself lost on the time sink called the internet, watching videos on weight loss and intermittent fasting. Other times, inspecting myself in the mirror, I think: 'Okay, now next week, detox week!'

And still, at others, I fantasise about enlisting a personal trainer, before the arrival of summer. Thinking, 'yeah that's all I need is a little push from a paid *friend*.'

I have no doubt that you know what I'm talking about. Don't be discouraged, however: they are simply thoughts, and thoughts can be subdued. The good news is with a bit of knowledge and self-love we can control our thoughts. In fact, we are the only ones who control our thought. We literally are what we think we are. I'll explain how to do that in this book.

Another challenge will be to become capable of tolerating and managing the people surrounding you. The rule of eradicating the superfluous also applies to friendships. However, we also live in a society, populated by humans, and most of all we want to learn how to deal with the continuous remarks and advice which, entirely unsolicited, people love to lavish upon us on a daily basis.

Sometimes I wished I could just snap my fingers and make everybody else go away. But then I figured it wouldn't be sustainable in the long term. I needed another method.

Some weeks ago, upon arrival in France following an extended work trip, a colleague observed me, smiling, and said, 'You look good. Whatever you're doing, keep it up.'

By reflex, I gave myself the up and down, particularly my legs, and cursed inwardly. Coming to my senses, I reminded myself that sure, this was not the first time, and nor would it be the last. Better to let it slide. Thankfully, over the age of 30, the armour thickens. It's one of the perks of aging.

Another challenge will be managing the visual input by social media and the media in general. What I'm about to tell you applies to Instagram, YouTube, Netflix and TV programmes. Let's say any type of transmission of images.

First and foremost, a cleansing of our social media. Social media gives us a very skewed picture of "reality". Therefore, this first step is obligatory in order to reach the physical form you desire. Instagram offers us a model of woman that belongs to another planet. I was born and raised in Italy. I have travelled half the world, and at this moment my time is split between France and Belgium, and I have still yet to see a living breathing woman who looks as perfect as an Instagram model image. There is no such thing as real time photoshop.

Hence, if you have tried everything and suspect that no diet is capable of making you a siren-haired giraffe with the breasts of Pamela Anderson, heed my words, start the process of unfollowing. If you want good examples say yes to those profiles of Beyonce, Ashley Graham, Alicia Keys, Taryn Brumfitt. There's a world of "normal" sized models to be followed, you just have to get out there and look. Despite your current weight and regardless of your ideal weight, these are the women to follow. It's worth reflecting and reassuring yourself of the fact that there are women of humane sizing, that are stunning, and that society and the public accept.

If you assume this is simply a detail, you are mistaken, for it is not. Every day we are bombarded with images which our subconscious translates into strong feelings of inadequacy. The overwhelming majority of stars that we observe on social media go to their plastic surgeon with almost the same frequency that we wash our hands, and yet they declare the secret of their beauty to be nothing more than: clean living, a glass of lemon water, plenty of sport and eight hours of sleep. On top of that, we then have to deal with the brazen: women of 60 years, without a line, a crease, a wrinkle, claiming that their youthful appearance is solely owing to the attention of their toy-boy.

Ignoring the fact that I find the idea of the miraculous water or the weight-eliminating sleep rather fascinating, it makes me pause and reflect on the message, because the majority of women and young girls that have to face these portrayed images reflexively feel inadequate, without considering how much time the aspiring Benjamin Button in question actually passed on the operating table or has been e-corrected.

Hence, once the social media cleanse is done, I advise it be used in a much more diminished fashion, and for various reasons reducing it to the essentials and creating a blank slate for ourselves. Remember what you see on social media isn't actual life. It's time for a new start. New content to follow could be vegetarian blogs, cooking courses, female empowerment, animal welfare, ping pong, whatever your interests may be, provided you don't fall again into the trap of following people who are physically incomparable with human beings: it will only reawaken your sense of inadequacy. The world is how we decide to see it. Our reality is what we believe it is.

My second recommendation is: have prepared some standard phrases, to be used in response to the comments from others. Note: 'please drop dead at my feet' should not be one of these phrases no matter how tempting it might be for you to utter those words. I've noticed that it is the habit of some to greet us with: 'You look fabulous, have you lost weight?'

However much you want to remind this person that considering the repetition of this greeting, by now you should've disappeared from the face of the earth, keep your cool and respond with: 'Thanks, you look great too.'

For me, because of my love of animals, I respond with: 'Oh thanks, since I stopped eating animals, I feel great'.

Other phrases to consider: "I feel great too!"

'Thanks, I'm happy.'

Or simply, 'Oh, thank you.'

What am I trying to tell you? That it is expected that most people will comment on your physical form. It's kind of human nature. Be it thin, tall, short, blonde, or dark haired. Because of this, it's better to not let yourself be influenced by the comments and respond with a phrase that makes ourselves feel better, first and foremost.

Another response I use is: 'Thanks, it's important to me that I take care of my health.'

In short, make use of responses that help you to feel at ease and if you can, that sidestep the original question asked. A little bit like in politics: vocalise your ideas, ignoring the questions of the journalist. Pretty much dance around the original question and respond how you like with something that makes you feel better.

Your constantly dieting friends constitute another problem altogether. You may tell the truth to your closest: that you are starting a detox from dieting, it will bring you to a place of mental and physical wellness, and you don't want to hear a word uttered on the subject of diets or self-criticism in your presence. I suggest you add that for you, they are beautiful exactly as they are, but I doubt they will believe you.

Some will listen to you, others, not having this ability, will continue to tell you: 'from tomorrow, back on the diet', while swallowing the first mouthful of lunch. '

I absolutely have to lose weight', 'look how fat I am', 'I have to start those massages' – I could go on forever.

We seriously underestimate the impact these negative messages have on our lives. It's a bit like passive smoking: those in contact with smokers are exposed to health risks, whether they choose to be or not. Until now, it was a vicious circle, fed by both parties, but now you have the knowledge and power to break this circle.

From today on, you have the power to withdraw from this madness or at least be conscious of the damage this type of behaviour can cause. You can try to separate yourself by setting boundaries and hoping your questioner, defeated, will go and complain to those who still indulge in feeling sorry for themselves.

You are no longer that person, or at the very least, you are working on it. The dialogues we conduct with ourselves make up the soundtrack of our daily lives. Our thoughts have a crucial role regarding the events, the choices and the people that take part in our lives. Our past represents the lens through which we observe ourselves, and how we interpret the happenings in our lives. Our thoughts, instead, constitute the voice of our Jiminy Cricket and accompany those events, determining how we feel and react during the course of our day, and consequently, the course of our lives.

Our Jiminy Cricket, if not tamed, becomes rebellious, negative and cruel. His voice is capable of holding us in his power, dominating any other thought we have when we relate to ourselves. I remember, some time ago, at an art studio where I was painting at the time, a young woman never let pass an occasion to insult herself.

If she dropped her brush by mistake, she would utter words in a lowered voice, such as: 'What the heck am I doing'; 'Wake up'; 'I should have stayed at home, today is not my day.'

Her Jiminy Cricket spoke so loudly that even I could hear him. I don't remember the final outcomes of her art, but I clearly remember surprise surprise that she didn't like that either and started to criticise her own work.

Our life experiences are sculpted from our memories, thoughts and perceptions. If you are thinking, 'Poor girl, why be so hard on yourself for a painting made at such a beginner's level?'

I invite you to reflect on the fact that you also do it to yourself, to your legs, to your arms, or any other part of your body you have decided to let be taken hostage by your own mean Jiminy Cricket. A very dear friend, educated, physically very lovely and successful professionally, never ceased to speak badly of her legs. How much she hated them, how huge they were, how much she would have liked to have a different pair of legs. This was the soundtrack to every evening while we were preparing to go out in Dubai, every time we put on our swimsuits in Mykonos, and in London, while we walked the streets, talking. One day, exasperated, I decided to confront her Cricket. After all, there is only so much anybody can listen to about somebody else's legs. Tactfully, I suggested she show a bit more respect for her legs. They had, in fact, permitted her to do the most wonderful things: go walking, travelling, visiting, swimming and so on. They never complain, even if her feet balked occasionally about wearing heels. Those legs that we accuse and insult are the very same legs from our childhood.

Would you ever turn to your inner child (or any child) and say, 'You should hate your legs!'

If we don't defend our own creation, if we don't put ourselves on our own side, who will?

Whatever be the part of your body that you have bullied for years, come to this realisation: This is how you are, and this is how you will be at the end. Don't take this as a cynical point of view. In this case, some awareness can spur us to start a new relationship, and above all, a new type of dialogue, with our body. A positive dialogue. Trust me, I'm positive that being positive will make you feel better.

Chapter 2
The Gym

Let's move on to more burning issues, and to the word that inspires guilt in many women: the gym.

The moment you raise the concept of the gym is when you hear the most incredible excuses; our imagination grows wild and we are ready for any excuse to keep us from leaving the house and facing the spectre of sport. I've created and I've listened to the most extraordinary explanations: 'my back hurts', 'ah, my good work out clothing needs a washing', 'the stars aren't aligned properly'.

Yet the most recurrent phrase is: 'I don't have the time'.

Here, I would like to remind everyone, including myself, that the day is comprised of the same hours for all the earth's inhabitants and that, if people who run businesses, successful professionals or volunteers who work full-time, and despite a full schedule still find time to engage in physical activity, I'm sure that it is possible for all of us.

Having got that off my chest, seeing as I belong to the thought to be mythological category of half-woman/ half-bed, let me tell you how I came to find a method of being involved in physical activity, consistently and for pleasure.

The first objective is to make the gym a part of your routine. Humans love routines. The more we do something, the more it becomes a habit. The journey from the couch to the exercise bike is easier than you could possibly imagine.

The first step, obviously, is to find the right gym. Then of course join that gym. I recommend a nice one, airy, with windows and a nice atmosphere.

It seems important to know you are heading somewhere clean and pleasant. If you walk into the gym and the scent wants to make you dizzy you may not want to use this one. Then again, you may, as apparently people work up a good sweat here.

It all boils down to what you like. The good news is these days there are a lot of options. Sacrifice a few takeaways and a few dinners and invest in your health.

The next step is Netflix. Carry yourself to the gym with this thought: 'Today, I'll watch my favourite series there'. Start with 30 minutes on the bike, thoroughly hypnotised by *Black Mirror* or *Jane The Virgin*, and you won't even realise that you went in the first place. Instead of watching tv on the couch, watch it while doing some light aerobic exercise, without having to even break a much of a sweat. Repeat this routine three times a week for a month and your body and your mind will do the rest. The recurring psychological pattern of a person who, as with me, has been on a diet their whole lives is that of extremes. Either I go to the gym and do two hours of training to fatigue, or I sleep. I either starve myself or I binge. With me it used to be all or nothing. I start on Monday, or I never start at all. If I haven't gone yet this month, I'll start next month. This mechanism of constant procrastination makes us different from women who don't have problems with food and eating.

My advice to choose someone from within your close circle who I would define as "a normal woman". I chose my mother, who has no problems with food and never has, and wants to stay in shape because it's good for her health. Choose a friend, a relative, whoever you find. The important thing is that she is not aware of the concept of dieting and obsession with one's own body.

If you don't know anyone that would be fit for the job, imagine a woman like her and imitate her! This form of mental modelling can be very useful. Then, in any decision-making process about food or fitness, ask yourself: 'Would a normal person do this?' Being "normal" requires acting normally.

Therefore, would a normal person spend two depleting hours at the gym, every day for a period of time before quitting everything, then submit to a state of food restriction alternated by bingeing? I think not.

Would a normal person put themselves on a Ketogenic diet, with the accompanying bad breath, smelly urine and the increased risk of intestinal tumours? Absolutely not. Once the "30-minute-Netflix-and-cycle 3x per week" routine has been established, keep going until it becomes a habit.

Now listen, I know what you're thinking: "I'll lose weight following this plan? Isn't it better to trawl through Instagram for the latest news on the pineapple diet?"

To this, I can only respond with: *enough, stop deluding yourself.* You'll never be able to keep it up. Stop throwing away money and behave like the adult you are. All the diets you have already done are not enough? All the yo-yo-ing of your weight? You know that even if you started the pineapple diet, you would end up breaking it and bingeing in secret, ashamed, sad and defeated. Enough, you can become a normal person with a healthy physique. Follow this simple advice and you will have the key to serenity, and consequently and unexpectedly, an untroubled, lovely body. Carry with you, in life, only that which you wish to transmit. What goes around comes around even when dealing with yourself.

Once the Netflix-and cycle routine is a habit, move on to 30 minutes of cycling, and 10 minutes of walking on the treadmill. Repeat this program for another month. If you are feeling adventurous after this it won't hurt to add some weight training to your training. It will make your feel even more pumped. I know some women worry about developing big manly muscles but this won't happen unless you really want it to happen and even then it would take a lot of effort.

Paradoxically, I know the most difficult thing for you will be: not doing more. Normal people, faced with this idea, would be entirely confounded.

I imagine they might say: "Wait, you didn't want to get up off the couch, and now you want me to believe that you have an impelling desire to not do only more time but at a higher intensity?"

However, yes. We have lived lives of compulsive excess, and we need some time to get out of this habit. The wonderful thing is, the feeling that comes with the thought of never submitting to any kind of diet, ever again, is so heartening, so exciting, that it makes me want to open my balcony doors and shout it to the world: "I'm queen of the world!"

Chapter 3
The Kitchen

The kitchen is an important place, to be cherished and beautified. One recommendation I often give is that of decorating the fridge with colourful imagery that fills you with peace and joy. Postcards of flowers, photos of you with your loved ones and positive affirmations.

If you were one who had images of supermodels or of pigs or similar as a warning, get rid of it all immediately. From now on, the fridge is a friend. An ally that holds nutritious and delicious food at your disposal.

Personally, I like to embellish my fridge with positive phrases, addressed to myself, and to life. 'I am beautiful', 'Today I am calm and serene', 'I'm surrounded by people who love me and want the best for me', 'My life is exciting and full of surprises'. If you are a sci-fi fan you can add: 'the force is strong with me.'

Even if your goal, from today on, is that of reaching normalcy concerning food, I advise you to avoid keeping junk food around the house. I know that regular folk frequently keep Nutella in the cupboard and are not obsessed with it.

However, you and I will need time to reach that level. If you have kids, and you are "obliged" to buy treats as snacks, there are plenty of options that are healthy and at the same time delicious. Organic peanut butter, free of additives, on rice-cakes is an incredibly tasty substitute for chocolate biscuits, and is a snack that you can happily consume whenever you have the craving. Of course, fresh fruits and veggies can also be a great choice.

TIP: It's human instinct to see food and then want to eat that food. Keep food out of plain site. This has the added bonus of making your kitchen cleaner less cluttered. If you want to have something out leave a bowl of fresh fruit. Or maybe some celery and carrot sticks and some avocados.

After giving you this example, you might be thinking: 'This lady is nuts, (BTW nuts are a good choice) surely she knows how many calories there are in peanut butter?' But remember, I am speaking now to your Jiminy Cricket, and telling him that you are no longer on a diet, any diet. POOF it's gone, using the magic of the power of your mind. You've chosen to favour the method of eating what your body is asking for and eating to hunger. This method will revolutionise your life for the rest of your days.

Salads, ready-made quinoa, sugar-free non-dairy milks, avocado, vegetarian hamburgers, seitan steaks, seeds, almonds, oranges, lemons, pineapple, Brazil nuts, legume dough and pastas, sugar-free, unsalted organic peanut butter, falafel, buckwheat crackers, olive oil, nuts, linseed, sesame and hemp oils, peas, beans, sweet potatoes, brown rice, cashews, dark chocolate (yum), prunes, pomegranates, whipped linseed oil to substitute with eggs, peppers, etc.

All of these are foods that are healthy and nutritious, and that fill my shopping trolley with colour and vitamins. Ideally, we eat at least five different colours a day. (Yes, there may not be truly any blue foods but there are plenty of purples, greens, reds, yellows and oranges).

Personally, I don't eat meat, because the thought of eating living beings doesn't fill me with excitement, but if you can't do without it, try to buy organic fish, not farmed, or free-range chickens raised in the country. (Which is kind of obvious since it's hard to be free range in the city, plus people would complain.) The level of hormones contained in the poor beasts that we eat are harmful to our health and lead to weight gain. Eating meat can increase the risk of developing cancer, induce insulin-resistance (the first step towards diabetes), increase the risk of developing chronic cardiovascular illnesses, and, climate wise, has a catastrophic environmental impact.

(Note: I'm not a doctor. I don't even play one on TV. But also, this can be verified by browsing medical journals. Additionally, if you insist on eating some red meat and say things like "humans are carnivores". Remember our hunter gatherer ancestors ate the fruit and nuts from gathering far more often than they did meat from the hunt. Therefore, consider changing gradually your diet to discover how wonderful blood-free food is).

Beyond food, I advise always having healthy drinks in reach, particularly spring and sparkling water. Lemon, lime and orange go well in these: add thin slices to your water for added flavour. Lemon is a fantastic addition to the diet as it aids absorption of the iron contained in our food.

I also like using oranges for a refreshing and unique drink that I make whenever I have the desire. Add half a cup of orange juice to the same of sparkling water with a couple of drops of stevia for sweetness.

There's a lot you can do where a little effort and creativity goes a long way!

Chapter 4
Prohibited Foods

Once and for all let's put to rest the myth of fruit being high calorie, and that it contributes to weight gain. For 15 years I demonised fruits such as bananas or grapes, to the point that I almost forgot they existed. A recurring popular belief, endorsed mainly by dieticians, is that certain types of fruit should be banished due to their caloric content. On the contrary, fruit is an element of our diets that should undeniably be part of our daily intake. It is rich in minerals, vitamins, fibre and water. All of these things are vital to the human body. Avoiding them is silly. Furthermore, the fructose found in fruit is lower on the glycaemic index compared to the sugar that is produced industrially and is, without doubt, healthier when compared to the sweeteners found in many commercial low-calorie energy bars.

Having met with several dieticians, I wonder how on earth it's possible that none of them specialises in eating disorders. To me, it seems evident that those with weight problems, in the majority of cases, are also those carrying internalised suffering, a dissatisfaction regarding some aspect of their lives, that induces a tortured love/hate relationship with food and eating. They attempt to eat their problems away. It is certainly not the fault of, say, grapes not even those instruments playing California grapes.

Yet that is how it works: dieticians prohibit bananas instead of prohibiting that which is the actual, principal cause of weight gain. That is, the act of denying yourself, restriction, a sense of inferiority, sadness and solitude, these are the causes of or at the very least big contributors to weight gain.

Countless dieticians also condemn certain plant-based products, such as meat substitutes, asserting that in a weight loss diet, one must favour animal meat over soy or legume-based 'processed' vegetarian meats and products, as it is these that promote weight gain. Yet again, I am stunned by the predilection of putting meat before foods grown in our soil and rich in nutrients, regarding them simply in relation to their 'caloric content'.

A way of eating that is high in restriction and that goes on for a long time can only result in frustration sadness and an increase in weight. Sandra Aamodt, a neuroscientist hailing from the United States, explains in her TED talk that diets, in the majority of cases, do not work, simply because hunger is driven chiefly by the mind.

To put it very simply: often we 'see food we want to eat food'. These are urges that date back to when we were hunter gathers. We needed to snap up food when we found it since we didn't know when our next meal would be. Civilisation has made finding food much much easier. You can even summon it with a phone in your pocket. Just our brains haven't caught up with technology.

On a side note, I do wish more dieticians, trainers and weight consultants would learn and therefore share with their clients positive psychology techniques. After all, eating can be often triggered by feelings. Positive Psychology techniques can help stem this side effects of being humans.

As the name implies Positive Psychologists such as Dr Martin Seligman and Dr Barbara Fredickson help people to focus on the positive sides of life.

Basically, positive psychology attempts to get people to focus on the positive aspects of a situation. True there are some situations you can't take anything positive away from but these situations are far less common than most of us believe. Usually, you can control how you feel and react to any given event. To quote Harvard professor Dr Dan Gilbert in his "the surprising science of happiness" Ted Talk humans have the ability to synthesise happiness. We try to find happiness when really we can create our own happiness.

Some of happiness (around 40% is determined by our genes) another 10% is determined by a given situation.

The rest up to 50% is how we perceive and react to a situation. This part is under our control.

You can learn to build on and strengthen your control of your thoughts. Positive psychology helps to do that by fostering happiness. Ways to include widening social connections with family, friends and organisations or simply giving some your time to others. Giving almost always makes humans feel better. Happiness can also be increased by exercise and mediation and mindfulness. Just staying in the moment and concentrating on what you are doing now, can help.

Here's something simple you can do for yourself to help yourself feel better right now: just take a couple of deep breathes, in through the nose out through the mouth. Just relax on concentrate on your breath. See, don't you feel better now?

We do have a lot of control over how we feel. For example, think about how you feel right now. Now just look up, start jumping up and down and make yourself smile. Do you feel better? See the simple act of smiling makes us feel better. You do control over how you feel.

Chapter 5
A Judging Eye

After having eliminated, once and for all, the detritus of Instagram, it is now most important to start to train our eyes into seeing a new vision of beauty and femininity. Remember reality is what we believe it is. In most cases, as women, we tend to coldly compare ourselves with whomever we run into. (Well, not literally run into.) We see a woman and our brain, tragically focused on our own physical appearance, makes an account of the situation and brings us to a conclusion: 'I'd like to have her looks or her eyes or her knees', or to the other extreme, 'OMG! at least I don't look like that'. Whoever may be the chosen victim of this internal confabulation, it is essential to distance ourselves from this propensity that only puts us and others under pressure and severe scrutiny. That which will make you reach the ideal physical form is inner peace. Any type of tension whatsoever, which is under the control of ourselves or our internal dialogue, must be eliminated or at least greatly reduced or steered to a more positive course.

For years, I was the victim of comparison. I wondered how I appeared in the eyes of others compared to this or that other person rather they be in front of me in person or via social media. (Social media can be very unsocial-able.) For some time now, other than being free of the spectre of dieting, I've learned to monitor my thoughts and to eliminate many other poor habits. Habits that are not related to food and eating, but still have had a strong impact on reaching my desired physical form.

Now, every time I see a woman in the street, I practice being positive by identifying an external characteristic that I can appreciate. She is wearing a beautiful dress, has a calm air, gorgeous hair colour, fabulous earrings or nice knees, and I make sure to focus on those positive qualities. Practicing benevolence towards others will help you in finding it for yourself, and vice versa. Plus, being nice to others makes you feel better about yourself. Once again what goes around comes around.

I can't promise that it will be an easy path, however, on top of it being something sensible and worthy, it will also bring you much more than just physical wellbeing. The pathological focus on the way we eat, takes up space, and also leaves no room for many other things in our lives. Conversely, having natural eating habits and attitudes, based on our hunger, and eating simple and natural foods, gives us physical vitality and lucid mental acuity.

Your eating habits and your physical appearance can't and mustn't be the central focus of your life. They should be merely a side note amongst the many things we do during the course of the day and that contribute to our wellbeing.

For all of us, the day is made up of the same number of hours but if you dedicate your energy and your thoughts to fables about diet, your weight and your body, you're tossing away a lot of valuable hours.

Another fundamental principle that helped me reach a psychological serenity and with it, a physical equilibrium is that which I call "the principle of connected compartments".

Picture your mind divided into two compartments, and that these compartments communicate with one another. One is full of thoughts relative to dieting, calories, the urgency of losing weight, the need to rush frantically to the gym, frustration aimed at our appearance and a sense of impotence. In the other, we have empty space a void waiting to be filled.

Now, my advice is to cultivate this empty space, collecting all the thoughts relative to wellbeing, to serenity and peace, to spirituality, to calm, to breathing, to meditation, to relaxed and moderate physical exercise, to healthy and natural eating habits, to writing, reading, painting, to love, to making love, to helping others, etc. ... The objective is to make the compartment that is full of reassuring and positive thoughts start to overflow into the other. Bit by bit, as this happens, the "grey" thoughts will start to decrease in number and take on less and less importance ... until they disappear figuratively pushed out of your brain.

Disassociating yourself from annoying Jiminy Cricket also means the start of the discovery of other new passions. When I was immersed in the world of dieting, I was so focused on that aspect of my life, that if someone had asked me about my interests I wouldn't have had a clue how to respond. I might have mumbled, 'Ah, dieting ...'

A real conversation killer there.

Today I am constantly discovering what interests me because I have given my mind the space and the resources to think of other things, and above all, to get to know itself.

Unfortunately, if we cultivate the "grey" compartment of our mind, the thoughts of frustration will themselves start to overflow, filling our "positive" compartment and having a definitive effect on multiple aspects of our lives. Not by any mere chance, when I was dieting I was in an unhealthy relationship; sad, unhappy and frustrated.

The moment I started to follow the path of the diet detox, I met my prince charming, and, as if magic, I lost the kilos I had to spare. It seems utopian but I assure you that, like a domino effect, if you apply these simple concepts to your life, the result will be a chain reaction, proving itself when these small changes are repeated on a major scale and transforming everything in your life.

Abandon destructive thoughts related to dieting, fasting, x-day weight loss programs, weight loss products etc; be good to your mind, to your moods, to your body. Keep in mind that in order to have this project change your life and your physical appearance, it is extremely important to take care of yourself.

It is of fundamental importance to feel to be the best version of yourself today, not tomorrow. 'When I lose weight I'll get my haircut', 'There's no need for me to wax, I hardly wear a skirt', 'I won't put nail polish on, it's winter', 'When I've lost weight I'll go shopping and change my whole wardrobe'. 'It's no use getting those massages if I don't lose weight first', 'When I am the size I want to be, I'll buy some sexy lingerie', 'When I've lost this weight I'll be able to buy a two-piece, and have a great summer on the beach', 'When I've lost weight, I will finally deserve the man of my dreams'.

I know that these thoughts have continuously deafened you for years. I know that you, too, don't remember when and how they started. But above all, their message is: when you've lost the weight, that is, when you follow a diet to the end, you will finally be happy. This will never happen, you know it. Imagine being able to do everything I have just mentioned, not waiting for the day that will fatefully and mystically, suddenly change everything. You might as well have wished for a magical flying unicorn. Start being realistic. Start with the simplest things and take care of yourself today. Make an appointment with your beautician or do it yourself. Give yourself a makeover. Enjoy yourself, take care of the body that for so long you have belittled or ignored. It's the only body you have and that you'll ever have for this is the only life you'll live.

(I know you might be thinking: wait aren't google and Elon Musk looking for ways to transfer our minds into computers or clones or something like that. But even if by some miracle this happened, would you really want to leave your fate to a company that tracks everything you do or another one that launches cars into space just for fun?)

Your age and your financial status are irrelevant. If you have limited economic resources, shampoo more often, do some hair removal, moisturise, put on foundation, mascara and concealer every day. There are brands for every budget with reasonable prices, found at the supermarket, with which you can treat yourself.

If you are a little better off financially, invest in a round of massage treatments or pressure therapy to feel lighter and improve your blood circulation.

Let's start enjoyable beauty routines without waiting another day. You deserve it! As soon as you wake up in the morning, spend 10 minutes on your looks. Put on some make-up, wash your hair, shave, moisturise and take care of your body. That body which we decided to punish simply because it rebelled from the proscribed "50 grams of brown rice for lunch". When you think about it, it sounds a bit nuts, doesn't it? Heck, nuts would be much better.

We often speak of altruism, generosity, doing well, respecting others. Let's start first with ourselves, and cherish our bodies as if they were a being that had been deprived of many things and, principally, love. It's easier to love others when you love yourself.

Chapter 6
It Depends on The Weight

Following my senior experience with extreme weight loss programmes, I am finally happy to share the formula that I know without a doubt will improve, whatever be your current physical form. It's no easy achievement to break the cycle of pathological attachment to food as a means of comfort.

Furthermore, your mind is always prepared to accept any excuse to be comforted by the idea of the miraculous diet. Humans are really good at finding ways to justify their actions now and in the past. That's where the saying "the good old days" comes from. We are actually living in an amazing time now: people living longer than ever, we can cure many diseases, we have access to travel and information our grandparents would consider the stuff of science fiction.

When I first shared my ideas about the importance of peace with oneself, and a way of eating that incorporates natural, plant-based foods to a close friend, who had been on a diet her entire adult life, she responded in defence of the weight loss diet, which never works and indeed never had for her.

She said: 'Yeah, maybe for someone who only has to lose a few kilos, but you know I have a lot of them to lose. I need to be on a diet, it's a question of my health.'

It seems incredible, but that's the way it is. Old habits truly can be very hard to break. I, too, believed for years that the 50-grams-of-brown rice-for-lunch weight loss diets were the right track because it was "prescribed" to me by a doctor.

I then became aware that that doctor had never had any kind of eating disorder or a problematic relationship with food. If they had and if they had resolved it, undoubtedly they would have never been able to speak to anyone on the topic of weighing food and banishing bananas. Plus, for that matter medical doctors have very little training in diet and good eating habits.

Television programs investigating obesity and interviewing the morbidly obese clearly unmask the difficulty of these people's relationships with food and following weight loss diets: they report the desire to consume food, to eat in secret, to stress eat, to eat to celebrate and for joy, to eat to deal with anxiety. In short, that which we call emotional eating.

Take this news, that you will never subject yourself to a diet again, with enthusiasm rather than dejection, and realise you really don't have a choice. Which is better: a good dose of reality and the achievement, little by little, of an improvement in physique and a body weight that is healthy, or continuing to suffer through ups and downs, off yo-yo or boomerang diets with short term plans and an increasing stockpile of delusions? I think you know which. Picture yourself emptying your mind of all tensions relating to your figure and opening to a world of opportunity and potential.

Your poor brain, having constantly been harassed by dietary messages, unrealistic images and guilt, has convinced itself that it is trapped in a bitter tasting stalemate. Not allowing your mind, the space to breathe stops it from being capable of making progress in other areas of your life. Do you really want to reach the ripe old age of ninety, thinking: 'Ah, they've come up with a new diet! This time I'll going to do it!'? I think not. I personally lived through this mindset for fifteen years, how long has it been for you?

Here's a technique you can use to change a bad habit to a good habit or to reach a goal you have. It's a technique called:

Wish Outcome Obstacle Plan

or WOOP for short.

WOOP was developed by Dr Gabriele Oettigen, Professor of Psychology at NYU.

WOOP is easy to use and can be a useful tool to add to your life improvement tool box. WOOP (as you've probably guessed) comes in four steps. You need about 5 minutes of calm and quiet to start WOOPing.

Step one: The Wish. Find something about yourself that you wish to change or improve. The wish should be something you can truly accomplish over the next days or months. It should also be something you find important. Plus, it need to be challenging. Then sum up this wish in 3–6 words. For instance I have a friend who used WOOP. Their wish was "eat more fruits & veggies, less sweets."

Step two: The Outcome. Envision your best outcome. Think about how that outcome will make you feel. Imagine yourself feeling that way. Summarise the outcome in 3–6 words. Image it again until you can feel the change. My friend's outcome was: "Lose weight and feel better."

Step three: The Obstacle. Turns out this is an important step. You need to think about what could block you from achieving this outcome. What is the main inner obstacle. Then some this up in 3–6 words. For my friend it was, "I really like eating sweets."

Step four: The Plan. You plan what to do to get around this obstacle. Summarise that in, you guessed it, 3–6 words. For my friend it was: "eat veggies & fruits instead of sweets." Then you set up and if [obstacle] then [action to overcome obstacle.

For my friend if [I want sweets] then I will [eats veggies and fruits.]

This helped my friend lose a couple pounds a month and feel healthier.

You can learn more about WOOP at woopmylife.org. They even have an app for that.

Chapter 7
The Detox of The Tongue

You've heard of detoxing in the context of food and of eating, of toxins and of the colon, yet very few words are spoken on the subject of the detoxification of our language.

Astonished? How is it you've heard of every type of detox but not of this verbal one? How is it possible that this one flew under your diet-radar?

We are fixated on what we put in our mouth. What we eat, what we drink, what we breathe. Yet very little attention is given to what comes out. The words we utter are the musical accompaniment to our daily choices and outlook. Words may not physically hurt but they can do harm nevertheless.

Awaking to see a glorious day bathed in sunshine, and choosing music to listen to while you shower for work, I have trouble believing you'd choose the funeral march or some other grim tune. You'd choose a song that invokes the sunshine, positivity, celebration, love and liberty. Just this morning, I was listening and singing to Queen's *Don't stop me now.*

Imagine that with the words that exit your mouth, you create music. Sadly, I don't think that every morning you greet your neighbour with: 'I'm great, thanks! The sun is shining, I'm certain that I'll live out today as if it were a day of celebration. I'm in love with life, and I'm lucky to be a free woman living in the me-too era!' Instead, most commonly I'll hear: 'Yeah, I'm alright, I guess, you make do with what you've got. It's nice enough today, but they say that it's going to rain all next week. Today will be difficult as I've got so much on my plate: I can't wait until it's the weekend.'

I'm sorry to be the bearer of bad news, but listening to you is like hearing the death march played by bagpipes instead of a song of celebration. It's a sad melody that reverberates through all aspects of your life, including your body.

As Tony Robbins, master of communication and the achievement of personal objectives, says: the secret of reaching an objective is to condition ourselves. In cases like ours, this conditioning involves cultivating thoughts we would like to have dominate our day and, if serenity is the key to dealing with an emotion-based eating disorder, the melody of our day must be based on words that evoke fulfilment and tranquillity.

Try practicing a state of calm, allowing yourself to really, emotionally, feel it. Try saying: 'Today I feel incredibly peaceful, how wonderful! I love feeling at one with the world.' Remember to keep breathing in and out (it's amazing how easy it is to forget to breath) tell yourself to breath in slowly from the diaphragm and then to let the air out. While breathing concentrate on your or the words. Picture them in your brain if you like. Breath in and out a few times.

Stay in the moment of now. Let the world around you fade away. It's surprising the effect this carries over into your body … not a single diet exists that can equally compare with this sensation. In your conversations of the coming days, including today, simply take note of what you're saying. Listen to the people around you. How many people are singing songs of joy, and how many are producing funeral renditions? Ignore the later. Try to emulate the former. We really are what we think we are.

These days, we mistake negativity and complaints as being synonymous to conversation.

'Packing your bags for holidays is a nightmare', 'This weather is horrible', 'This traffic is frightful', 'I'm buried in work', 'I'm dead tired,' 'My boss is a twit!'

The real challenge in obtaining a healthy figure and mind, after having realised how much negativity that you expose people to and are exposed to, is changing your behaviour, and starting the purification of toxic language and expression.

As the syllogism of Aristotle teaches us: if it is true that the detoxification of language leads us to a state of serenity and that serenity then leads to a healthy weight, it is therefore true that detoxification of language is an analogous process that has the same outcome of success. Or to put it simply think good positive thoughts and positive things happen.

I here want to specify that the process described in this book for achieving a healthy body must be read and reread as many times as possible, almost as if it were a magical text with ever-changing content. (Which it may very be.) Reading it twice isn't enough, repeat it a third and a fourth time.

That we read it is in fact not as important as when we read it. When you think you've understood the mechanism and that you're at a good point in your physical transformation, come back to these pages again.

As you become familiar with this new lifestyle, you will grasp new concepts that have remained hazy in past readings. It's a similar process as that of when you first become aware of a certain something and suddenly, you see it everywhere. It has always been there but it had never previously grabbed your attention.

It's important that you know that despite the effort you put into the language detox, there will be people who have not read this book, and never will. As with any important change, you will be forced to make choices. Relations with people who aren't capable of welcoming milder language should be kept to a minimum. If they are unavoidable relationships, such as with a partner or a colleague and they haven't had the fortune of discovering this new way of being, then it will be up to you to provide a good example and introduce positive and harmonious language.

You'll begin to notice that following your umpteenth joyful response to their complaints, they'll vent to someone else. Or maybe, dare I say it, start to change themselves.

A fundamental rule of the language detox is to never, and I mean never, gossip. Yes, gossip might be fun and make you feel better or superior in the short run but it's hurting you in the long run. We want to be positive with ourselves and others.

What does this have to do with the achievement of your ideal body? Everything. If you have something to say about the lives of others it means you've reached all your personal objectives, all your dreams have come true, your projects accomplished, you've read all the books in the world ever written and seen every film as well. Perhaps I'm being a little extreme with the concept but it's on this which I want you to reflect: your time could be used in a much more productive manner.

If you actually are concerned that someone has a problem, don't gossip about it. If you're so interested, you should find a way to help that person, not throw them under the bus to make yourself look superior. If you really were, you wouldn't need to talk about the lives of others.

Furthermore, in denigrating others, we denigrate ourselves. What goes around really does come around. On the other hand, if we help, if we do good, if we rejoice in the victories of others as if they were our own, we only inspire joy and positivity within our own experience. This ability, however, cannot be developed overnight. Envy is, after all, a human emotion but we can work on managing and training it until we free ourselves from it. How? We start by being conscious. Observing ourselves and others is the first step towards effective change.

If you are thinking: 'No, this doesn't ring true for me, I'm not a jealous type of person'.

I ask you to ask yourself: is that really true? Don't feel guilty if you're overcome by strange feelings when a colleague of yours gets a major promotion, or if a friend is marrying an incredible man while you're on the hunt for someone to go out with on a Saturday night. There's nothing wrong, we're human beings. We're not perfect.

The good news is we're not made of stone either our brains are elastic. We have the means and the ability to over-write these feelings and make room for opposing sensations. We truly are what we think we are. And we can control what we think but like anything else in life it takes practice. If, it happens that you comment on other women, defining and judging them, then this chapter is written for you: read it until you know it by heart.

'Look how slim she is', 'She's very brave to be dressing like that', 'And I thought it was me that should be losing weight', 'Poor thing, she's so flat I've seen better built boys' – these are phrases that should raise the alarm.

If you are a heterosexual woman, stop looking at the women that pass you, it's counterproductive no good can come from comparing yourself negatively with others or putting others down to improve how you feel. If you're surrounded by people who make these kinds of comments, with pity and compassion turn to them and answer: 'Come on, let's focus on you? Is everything okay? You seem tense'.

With this, they'll realise that they are not in the kind of advantageous position required for these kinds of comments and spite. And quite frankly nobody should be judging others, except of course for judges. We can now start a phase of improvement that will create room only for hope and progress. Something else that characterises this process of evolution is, lo and behold, learning to accept a compliment.

Most of the time, when someone compliments us on our outfit or our appearance, we freeze. Panicked, we immediately wonder about the sincerity of this person, or if they had, in fact, left the house without their glasses. To: 'You look splendid!' We respond indignantly, with: 'Get out of here, I didn't get any sleep at all last night and my eyes are hanging down to my knees'. 'What a gorgeous dress' elicits: 'Yes, it's nice isn't it, I just have to lose weight'. 'Beautiful earrings!', 'They're only from the market, I paid about 4 euros'. 'I love your hair', 'It needs a cut, I have split ends'. 'Hey, congratulations on your new job!', 'I reckon it'll be quite difficult'.

I could write an encyclopaedia of self-destructive responses. None of them at all useful.

I wonder what it is that stops us from responding proudly and with joy: 'Thanks, I love this dress, it makes me feel marvellous, and I, too, love my hair'.

First of all, we aren't used to such self-congratulatory conversation because, as we've seen previously, negative expressions make up the current language and remain stubbornly used in daily speech. Further, and probably more importantly we don't feel up to the standard of being praised. After all, if we insult ourselves, how could we permit a stranger to do otherwise?

The environment surrounding us is the result of the beliefs that have been sung to us by our Jiminy Cricket for the majority of our adulthood. If the voices inside you, along with your thoughts, judge your appearance by the standards of the weight loss diet theory or social media, you'll take every occasion and any remark to nourish your feelings of inadequacy. You're a good-for-nothing owing to the fact you can't stick to a starvation diet and become as thin as possible. No occasion or circumstance is accepted: holidays, going out to dinner: the cricket is always watching, disgusted, and to be honest … it's a shame. It's as if we've decided to live under a self-created dictatorship, without even thinking about all the infinite qualities with which we came to this earth.

A fundamental thing to recognise is that we have time to change, whatever be our age. My mother and her friends, in their sixties, often speak about how to improve themselves, accept themselves and enjoy life whilst treating themselves with as much understanding, mercy and compassion as possible. It's never too late to quiet our cricket. We can modify our previously consolidated habits by following some simple tips, and as I love to repeat, the first step towards change is awareness. In short, that you are reading these words, means you're halfway there. And the achievement of a healthy physique is closer than you think.

I adore the metaphor of the labyrinth. Picture yourselves having been trapped within one for years and being finally two steps away from escape. Going back would mean being trapped forever in a world of illusions (dieting), false exits, doors that give way only to more doors or brick walls or maybe even reveal a hungry tiger. You can happily turn back, and download the slimming tea diet from Instagram, but you are just as free to make those last two steps and exit, hair flowing in the breeze, out into the world of normal and balanced people. Once you've taken those last two steps, you'll never turn back. Every now and then, you'll think about that good old labyrinth with nostalgia, and some memories will come back to you. But by now, you're done with it, and the feeling of liberation is without comparison.

Chapter 8
The Detox of The Ears

As you would imagine, if the language detox/ detox of the tongue requires filtering and purifying the words that come out of us, the audio/tongue/mouth detox is just as important. The power of this detox needs to be publicised. Everyone should be informed of the effects, particularly those that are negative, that the messages we listen to could have in our lives. Media, for example, comprises a veritable source of passive listening, and reality shows, like many other forms of trash transmission, should come with a disclaimer: 'known to kill neurons and intelligent thoughts and lower IQ' – as of that for cigarettes. If you don't believe me talk to somebody who regularly watches say BBC News. A lot of their views will be heavily slanted towards the "news" they are fed on that channel.

I remember having read a book written by the wife of the renowned American entrepreneur Grant Cardone and being left stunned by the stories of the frequent, sudden fights between them. She then realised that she had been following a reality show for quite a while, Beverly Hills Housewives, and she became aware of how much stress, screaming and unhealthy ideas that program had brought into their home.

That reality show became their reality. Their fights, in fact, centred upon the very same themes being dealt with in the show. From the moment they stopped watching the series, the fights magically ceased. I wonder: What are the models upon which we mould ourselves? By whom are we letting ourselves be influenced? Maybe there should be a reality show about people who do selfless deeds. Or maybe one on positive psychology? More on positive psychology can be found at The Positive Psychology Centre: ppc.sas.upenn.edu.

When a song is played on the radio for the first or even second time, it's impossible for us to immediately recall the lyrics. However, in listening to the song over and over for an hour, most days of the week, religiously, you'll learn those words by heart.

Even if you aren't trying. If you're thinking: 'Who cares, after all, they're only the lyrics of a song and it's just entertainment or an ear worm that won't go away. How weak are those who let themselves be influenced by a reality show', you are in total denial. It's a process that is carried out on a subconscious level.

In short, when a message is listened to again and again and again, it becomes assimilated in our psyche. Think about advertising, even the crudest form of publicity is based on the principle of repetition, leading the listener to mentally repeat the slogan, and then it's game over.

This argument, of course, goes for Facebook, Instagram, and vlogs. Don't make social media your reality. Remember what you see on social media isn't a true slice of somebody else's reality. It's a very skewed look into their world. Very few people post bad things about themselves on social media.

You never see a picture of a person stubbing their toe or a fighting with their mate. Or see a person when they first wake up into the morning. You only seeing them at their best: having fun, looking great, or being the ideal family.

Nobody ever says, "Oh I look terrible in that shot. Let's post it to Instagram."

This is all fine and good if you don't compare your entire life to the very filtered lives of others you see on social media. Remember what you see on social media is a very veiled slice intro somebody else's life. They are only showing you the good things. They don't always look like alien-models, they aren't always in ecstaticity.

Don't compare yourself to what you see there. You have the same positive fun moments in your life too.

Use social media to fulfil a purpose: they are a means that should serve you, and vice versa. Try to spread positive views or news.

Banish reality TV and useless and superficial programmes: I'm certain you know how to recognise them. Quite frankly if something has "real" in the title, it's not. In this era of *Apple,* we can now access more varied and interesting concepts. Podcasts and audiobooks can keep us company on our commutes, long trips, walks in the park and during our workouts.

Conversations on art, cooking, health, success, fashion, politics, economy, sport, travel, history; the possibilities are infinite. If you don't know what I'm talking about, look it up on the web – Google is your friend. Then, we have alternative cinema and immediate access to film and series on Netflix, where you can choose from hundreds of art house films and interesting programmes.

If you think you're in the wrong age range for these things, you're mistaken. The age limit was invented solely to excuse one's own laziness. Ask your children, your grandchildren, your nieces and nephews, a neighbour, or take yourself to the nearest department store, where I'm sure you'll find a young one (age-wise) happy to help you. Use modern technology, you'll see it's easy and intuitive, all it takes is a bit of initiative and some help starting out.

A gradual method of eliminating the presence of trash programmes in your life is to try to identify your evening habits and be conscious of them. You can ask yourself: 'Do I really want the last imagery of my day, the last concept that I listen to, to be vapid and rambling?'. Hopefully you will answer, 'Now that I think about it, nope that doesn't sound healthy or much fun ...'

The influence of being a passive audience to rubbish TV programmes takes us a step further away from inner serenity and the achievement of physical equilibrium. As with every habit we keep in our lives, in order for it to be uprooted it must be replaced with another, more interesting alternative, and gradually. When you go back to watching stupid programmes, ask yourself if you really had the impetus to watch them, or if it was solely by automatic habit. Then tell yourself, 'there is probably something else I can watch that's just as entertaining with a much more positive message?'

I hope I've been able to plant the seed of awareness in an area of our lives whose effect is often undervalued, yet has strong counterproductive potential. Let's see if the idea blooms. Turn off the TV and turn on your audiobook, it'll keep you company and will be more pleasurable than you thought. I was completely addicted to an Italian trash TV show on courting, characterised by screaming and nonsense. I started to watch it when I came home every day from high school, it then became a habit that held me in its grip for a decade. How many are the things in our lives that are left-over from the past, and don't make any sense to keep in the present? And may have never made sense at all. Imagine if, at home, you hoarded all your clothes and keepsakes that you bought when you were an adolescent: you wouldn't even be able to open the front door. Of course, they may make one of the TV shows about you but would you really want the world looking at you saying, 'wow I'm glad I'm not that messed up.' I think not. You'd much rather influence the world with something positive and fresh.

Our mind needs a refresh. Let's put the house of our mind in order, throw out the useless objects and dust the furniture that's overflowing with knick-knacks. We have a lot of work to do but if we roll up our sleeves, one room at a time, the house will become as new!

Chapter 9
One Thing at A Time:
Little by Little

In my daily vocabulary, an expression is frequently repeated as if it were an interjection: 'little by little'. With these words, I express that I'm doing the work, I'm committing myself and I want to evolve; one aspect of my life at a time.

I'm giving you the same advice. Reread this book over and over again, until you have assimilated the concepts here presented. Put them into practice: be patient and loving with yourself. You'll fall into some relapses, you'll take some steps back, but realise that you are already far, far down the track from the starting line. Where you arrive, I have no doubt, will be much further than you could ever imagine!

The strategy of the achievement of your ideal body is to simply ignore the omnipresent and authoritative weight loss diet culture, and cultivate other aspects of your life.

Those which will make you come alive and transmit a sense of inner peace and fulfilment that, gradually, will extinguish the sedating and comforting powers of food.

I've spoken to you about the importance of consuming natural, and if possible, vegetarian foods. Not contributing to the killing of living beings can bring you a sense of peace in your life. Think about the fact that, based solely on the rule of harvesting that which seeds, you'll experience a wave of positive events in your life, owing to not being a part of the industry that causes death and suffering. Propagate life, harvest life.

If the world of vegetarianism or veganism is unfamiliar to you, and you are under the impression that not eating meat then means feeding yourself a diet of plain broccoli, you are greatly mistaken. I personally feed myself with nutritious, delicious, natural food, and when I have the desire for junk food I let loose with vegan hamburgers, pizza with chips and sausage and vegan ice-cream. If somehow you're new to this world, know that, in any big supermarket, you have access to substitutions for any type of food, simply ask. String cheese, sausages, meatballs, yoghurt, butter, mayonnaise and meatloaf don't necessarily have to be from the animal industry. Try the infinite variety of vegetarian products and choose your favourites.

To those who would comment with: 'I would imagine that these products are full of preservatives?', you can respond that, for years, you've eaten corpses in a state of decomposition, and you're sure that you are capable of taking this risk.

BTW, Oreos are vegan.

You'll hear it from everyone and their mother. When you dieted: 'Why aren't you eating? Come on, just try it …' on the other hand if you aren't on a diet: 'How come you never think of dieting?', if you're omnivorous: 'You'll die of a tumour', if you're vegan: 'You're missing your protein'. It is important to keep in mind that most people are ready to talk about anything and anyone so as not to approach and examine the most inflammatory subject of all: themselves. It's easier for them to criticise you. Therefore, focus on your goals and respond to people with patience and awareness, remembering the indisputable fact that this is your life path and it carries on independent of the choices and decisions of others. Be positive and encourage others to be positive around you with phrases like, 'doing this makes me feel better', 'I appreciate your input but I am happy this way!' 'Thank you for thinking of me, but I am happy. I hope you are too!' Stronger, more stubborn and more insistent than that of the people around you will be the obstacle that is your talking cricket. Like a capricious child in search of attention, he will never bore you.

The best thing will be, though, that from now on it may be that instead of rushing to make him happy, you decide not to pay him any attention, and make him understand that this time around, you take control of events. Or work on changing what makes him happy by being positive with yourself and not judging yourself. This cricket is not an old dog, it can be taught new mental tricks.

People like you and I have been forced, through circumstances, to become experts on dieting and slimming programs, so why don't we get excited about a way of eating, a plant-based one, that far from being characterised by awareness of calories and weight loss, instead confronts ethical and moral causes? It's an ideal substitute, one that will bring you joy and keep you busy in the discovery of a new culinary world. Light chocolate vegan pancakes, Buddha Bowls, peanut butter filled dates, nori wraps, stuffed sweet potatoes, lentil meatballs, the choices are infinite and delicious. Whether you love cooking or you're a fan of 5-

minute food, YouTube is your best ally, with healthy and delicious videos explaining all.

Chapter 10
The World Doesn't
Revolve Around You

In a society that is strongly focused on individualism, I here would like to remind you, like a bolt from the blue, that the world does not revolve around you. Far from wanting to be a defeatist, I am certain that conflicted relationships with food cause pathological self-centeredness, which, like a dog chasing its tail, is a factor that progressively fosters binge-eating disorders.

A tip that will help you break this vicious circle and achieve a balanced and healthy physicality is to dedicate a portion of your time to someone other than that being who looks at you in the mirror every morning. Be it helping out at your church, at a soup kitchen, making sandwiches at home to be handed out to the homeless in your neighbourhood or simply helping someone, anyone. Someone weighed down with shopping bags, the elderly who need help crossing the street, visiting someone who suffers from solitude. The ways of doing good are multiple, but absolutely exclude that of making donations. However honourable it may make you, a one-click payment on PayPal unfortunately doesn't contribute positively to the exit from the tunnel of exclusivism.

Studies have shown donating your time to people in need can increase your happiness more than buying something for yourself. Humans are pack animals and we seem to really mentally benefit by helping other members of our pack.

Chapter 11
Carrying the Torch

That the motivation is to carry out stable and lasting changes in your life is one of the most searched questions on Google: 'How do I find the motivation to lose weight', 'how can I make my dreams a reality', 'how do I end a toxic relationship'.

Really you should be looking at yourself not Google for this.

Often, in the course of a life, we are searching for our North Star. A point on the map, on which we can land safe and sound, which guides us to the end of suffering. In the case of the search of psycho-physical balance, motivation is the supporting structure of this impetus, of the instinct to change and evolve towards our best.

For years, I asked myself what was the mysterious force that could finally convince my brain, and consequently my body, to remain faithful to the food scale and the tasteless food.

I passed hours and hours watching bodily transformations of women who, whilst carrying out their daily activities and being extremely overweight, were caught off guard at being chosen for a TV series of intense physical training. Faces of disbelief and emotional upset gave way to tears and cries of joy. The reactions of those women were caused not by the Adonis who announced himself as their personal trainer, but rather by the mirage of victory and the creation of hope. Finally, there was someone who was willing to listen to and guide them; someone ready to take on the ascent out of the obstacles and suffering. People must remember reality shows only show a very skewed and narrow picture of the reality they want to show you. Even if a reality is trying to capture real reality (a big if) reality changes by simply informing the participants they are being recorded. None of us act truly like ourselves when we know we are being recorded. The one thing that always intrigued me in programs of this format, was the fact that the majority of the people interviewed, constantly and without prompting, expressed the same ideas: 'I want to complete this passage and free myself from the discomfort of obesity, for my children and for the people close to me'. What did they really mean with this statement that seemed to be generated from their hearts, not their minds?

The search for a driving force is a fundamental element that leads us hopefully towards having a trusted inner ally. Demanding that our mind and body follow a dietary scheme that obliges us to eat as though we were part of a laboratory experiment, weighing and examining every single substance we ingest is counterproductive, no fun and, long term, ruinous.

The way to achieve worthy and long-lasting results, and the light at the end of the tunnel that beckons us forward during the process of this mental and physical transformation, is the image of the generational torch.

Imagine being an athlete and taking part in a relay race, where instead of a baton to pass to your teammate, you have a blazing torch. This torch has been passed down to you and now, determinedly observing the path before you, you begin your performance. You know you must pass it on to others, but you are also aware that the way in which you perform will produce decisive results for the final event: reaching the finish line. And so, like the relay race, our path in life is comprised of fragments of experiences and events that create determining changes for generational evolution. Like a puzzle that, starting with your ancestors, will be brought to a conclusion by the generations to come. What were the achievements that were brought about before your existence? What did your grandparents pass on when handing over the baton to your parents? What did they want to change? What, then, are your parents doing to improve their lives and therefore yours? Note we are shaped by our ancestors by both the genes they give us and the environment they create. Finding psychological serenity and making peace with our body is one of the changes we should be proud to impart. The sense of liberation in seeing anxiety and suffering burn away when held to the blazing generational torch constitutes the greatest motivation, in that any sense of inadequacy that has shadowed us since we can remember finishes with us.

This principle is applicable to any aspect of our lives, like the choice of our partner or that of our work. With this, I am not claiming to have the power to determine the salvation of future generations to come.

But I absolutely believe that it's entirely possible to contribute, proactively, to the imparting of a positive message.

Chapter 12
Remember Past Victories

We are survivors of countless episodes of discomfort and condemnation, whereby the shape of your body dictated your mood, your level of vitality and the way in which you interacted in society. We nostalgically fixate on the mini-skirt that we once wore with pride, yet today more resembles a hat. We wistfully recall the year in which we were in physical splendour … if only we could return that idyllic era! When will somebody invent a time machine?

But now, I really want you to think about those moments, about that divine year. Were you happy, truthfully? If you had that time machine, would you really, returning to that period to meet the "in shape" you, meet a woman who was completely satisfied? Or today, ensconced in the present, are you recounting a happy and carefree person who never actually existed? I fear instead that the actual you of that golden age was instead obsessed with the grams that still had to be lost, or the feeling of bloated-ness, a sign of the abundant meal of the previous evening. It's human tendency to rationalise and remember past events to make them better. It then becomes clear that the achievement of a healthy and balanced physique is due not to the ability to weigh foods and militantly follow orders, but rather by working on making the body and the MIND interact, for the achievement of psychological fulfilment. One productive way in which we can, instead, turn to the past with pride is by reawakening those memories of past victories. In those dark and difficult moments, fragility and impotence seemed to reign supreme. Looking back, in this case, can be extremely helpful, and provide serious moral support.

Try to think of all your victories, all the challenges you met, all the events that brought positivity to your life, all the times in which, overcome by discouragement and not believing in yourself, you were able to succeed regardless. When you finished a course of study, when you were hired for a job, when you did that language course, when you gave birth, when you helped your family, when you cooked that incredible dessert. Find those happy moments recreate them and hold them in your mind. Feel like you felt back then.

If you aren't able to recall any significant occasion carried out to the end with success, think of a small event. Think of, I don't know, when you put together furniture from Ikea. In those moments, you weren't sure you'd be able to, or that you could finish that which you'd decided to undertake, even though today you know you could have had more faith in yourself and in your abilities. In the end, you were capable of following through and succeeding. You can do it.

Chapter 13
Nurture the Blossoming of Your Self-Esteem

Reigning supreme at all times is a sense of inadequacy, caused by thoughts that, by tormenting our minds, make us feel eternally inadequate regardless of the circumstances, and there is no occasion that can make this insecurity waver. Our minds have a tendency to misfire. For instance our strongest intuitions are more often than not incorrect. Like I'd be so much happier if I lost 20 pounds. Very little of happiness is tied to our waist line. As for health benefits, according to Cornell University Professor of Nutritional Science Doctor David Levitsky, doesn't recommend losing more than 10 percent of your initial weight.

Our minds also don't think in absolutes, this is one of dangers of social media. We see beautiful people on social media and think "why can't I look like that?". Without thinking that that person who looks like that in a picture on the internet doesn't look like that either.

Also a lot of us tend to see our flaws more clearly than our strengths. We need to concentrate more on our good points. We do have them!

There are people in our world who see much more in us than the size of our jeans. A boyfriend, a parent or a dear friend will often encounter a cold wall of scepticism and incredulity whilst trying to offer us a compliment Where does this hostility that we bear come from? How on earth can we overcome it?

First of all, I want you to know this: no one else exists. I know you see them there in the flesh, but their existence influences solely their own existence, not yours. What I'm trying to tell you is that despite whatever image you have of yourself and your body, try, in any situation, event or person, to look for the overwhelming evidence that supports this theory. We all look for validation even if we need to make false assumptions to confirm that validation.

Our self-talk and our thoughts are representative of Jiminy Cricket and are often echoed fragments of the most difficult moments of our lives. Those negative events can shape us, in a way so stubborn and so difficult to ignore and remain imprinted and lasting, paradoxically even in the face of years of numerous positive experiences. We are wired to remember the negative more from way back when we were hunter gathers. Back then you could make one mistake like 'nah that wiggling in the bush is the wind not a lion' and that was it. It was evolutionarily better to be safer than sorry.

Negative thoughts are there in our minds, and it takes only the simplest solicitation for them to be awoken. Negative thoughts aren't totally useless. Sometimes it's good to reflect and understand that actions have consequences but we shouldn't be paralysed by this. Not many lions or tigers roaming around to eat us these days.

A college friend, of Asian origin, told me how, during her studies, she was often bullied for her almond-shaped eyes and her olive skin. After this confession, I understood the motives for which, every time she spoke on ethnicity, she felt scrutinised and reacted to the topic in an emotional way.

In the atmosphere of that multicultural environment, no one was inclined in the least to carry out discriminative discourse. And yet, negative associations were the roots of her strong reactions, as those thoughts lived on within her. Having lived that experience, it became her compass. One that guided her in her interpretation of events. Another friend, on a work break, came to me, grief-stricken, and told me that in a moment of greed she had gone and bought a chocolate bar from the office cafe. Caught in the act by her colleagues, she panicked and told them it was actually for her boss. She acted as if she had been caught stealing money from the homeless.

I'm sure that these accounts will have sparked the memory of similar events in your own life, of which you were the protagonist.

The first step in our growth is to free ourselves from the preconceptions we hold in our mind and in our awareness. The next time you find yourself reacting automatically or feeling wounded, try to distance yourself from the occurrence, remember that the others don't exist, and focus on what you believe you heard. That idea belongs to you, not to the other. If it were not so, how then could it make you feel so vulnerable? Why do you think you need to lose weight? Why do you want to change? I asked this question to various people around me in different settings: work, personal and aesthetic. We think we are unique yet we belong to the same species, we have a limited number of mental paradigms and ideologies to follow. We all have pretty much the same chromosomes. They follow this dynamic:

A. Why do you want to lose weight?

B. Because I have huge ankles.

A. Ok, why do you want thin ankles?

B. Because thin ankles are beautiful.

A. Well, why do you think thin ankles are beautiful?

B. Because my mother thought so.

A. How come she thought that?

B. Because society (the others) taught her that.

A. Who is society? Who are the others?

B. The newspapers, social media …

A. Right, but to me, that still seems fairly non-specific, because in my social media I have plus-size models, and fashion magazines are only a small percentage of publications in general. And they reflect even a smaller percentage of real life. I'm sure that you won't be fixated on your big ankles for years only because a small percentage of publications in the world and the people you follow on Instagram publish images of women with ankles different to yours? And also, can social media or a publication really belittle your ankles? If so, would you let them do it? The answer to that quite frankly should be, no of course not.

B. Yeah, I understand where you are going, but I am me. I think my ankles are huge.

A. Look, the others don't exist.

There's only us here, we only have our own view of things. Our ankles only appear how we decide to see them. Having arrived at the awareness that the others don't exist and that your Cricket is the only one responsible for the decisions that you make about your beliefs, we can see how to tame this rebellious creature, with whom we are destined to live like a marriage – for better or for worse. But let's concentrate on the "for better".

First of all, don't think of him as the enemy, he is not. He doesn't have the means of understanding how he should behave. We'll take these tortuous thoughts and, with patience, day by day, mould them towards what we want our beliefs to be. We can reshape this mould. Or if you wish, remould the mould. You've flagellated yourself for years for your physical form. You've tried everything and you are constantly in search of a miracle that could liberate you from this burden.

At some point, you even took part in a program that assigned points for each type of food, ending up with a calculator always in reach, almost as if you were a food bookkeeper, late with the end-of-year balance.

Now, reading this book, your talking cricket will be fully active. He will try his best to make you continue to live behind a blindfold, believing that one fine day you will find the motivation, follow a diet, go shopping and fit into the size of your dreams and miraculously maintain that physical form for the rest of your life.

With love and patience, explain to that dear little beast that you've decided to defend your body, to treat yourself well, to be healthy and to tell any magazine, that makes you doubt the beauty of your ankles, to go to hell.

Take this news, that you will never subject yourself to a diet again, with enthusiasm rather than dejection, and realise you really don't have a choice. Which is better: a good dose of reality and the achievement, little by little, of an improvement in physique and a body weight that is healthy, or continuing to suffer through ups and downs, with short term plans and an increasing stockpile of delusions? I think you know which.

Picture yourself emptying your mind of all tensions relating to your figure and opening to a world of opportunity and potential. Your poor brain, having constantly been harassed by dietary messages, unrealistic images and guilt, has convinced itself that it is trapped in a stalemate. Not allowing your mind the space to breathe stops it from being capable of making progress in other areas of your life. Once again remember to take time to breath. Even stopping just to breath and be calm a couple minutes a day can be a big help. Do you really want to reach the ripe old age of ninety, thinking: 'Ah, they've come up with a new diet! This time I know I'll succeed!'

I think not. I personally lived through this mindset for fifteen years, how long has it been for you?

A life that is problematic in regards to food and eating is often similar to a roller-coaster (but not as enjoyable): periods of meticulous programming of weight loss schemes, physical exertion and subscriptions to apps with alarms that go off every now and then, reminding you to jump up and down in order to burn off the salad you ate at lunch. This being then alternated by periods of depression, unease within oneself and a lack of motivation.

These unsustainable thoughts inevitably bring us to throw in the towel and immerse ourselves in an ecosystem of consolation: food, bed, duvet. It's Archimedes' ball that, forcefully submerged in the water, comes back with an unexpected force and gives us a black eye. 'I'm not a complicated person, I don't have so many crickets in my mind' is a response I often hear from people when I ask about their interests outside of work matters. Are you sure you don't have any? Or is it easier to put them aside to avoid risking failure and disappointment? Ask yourself if this is true. I suspect you think you've tried everything, but I bet that, at most, you've tried three types of sport and a couple of cooking courses.

Even if you've tried ten or fifteen different hobbies, in this world around you there is still an endless amount of creative options available to you, hundreds of options that give you the possibility of passing an hour with yourself without ending up googling "nasal feeding tube weight loss". Who knows, you may even find something that allows you to enjoy yourself. You may be wondering why it's so important to find an activity that you are passionate about.

The motives for this are many, and are fundamental to the achievement of well-being and physical equilibrium.

Experimenting with activities that allow you to express yourself freely will help raise awareness within you that you are not just the numbers on a scale. That, in the universe of a life of a woman there aren't just the galaxies of work, family obligations and food restrictions. Experimenting with a hobby and getting out of your comfort zone can enrich your life in unexpected ways and reduce the space dedicated to thoughts about weight loss. Putting aside the dieting mentality will bring well-being and depth to your life, and will one day allow you to discover a healthy and balanced body, swimming, meditating, cooking, acting, sewing, photography, reading, studying … the options are infinite. Don't be afraid to try anything. Don't worry what others think. Even if you try something and fail you learn from that failure. Look for the positive and stress that. Try and try again, you'll find that activity that makes time fly, and with it, the extra kilos. A variety of activities can really be the spice of life. Plus 30 minutes of physical activity a day makes us healthier (a study from Karolinska Institutet in Sweden) and happier (Physical Activity and Incident Depression: A meta-analysis … The American Journal of Psychiatry).

Chapter 14
Break Stress into Pieces

Employers, wives, employees, mothers, students: we seem to be taking on more and more roles, simultaneously. Added to the usual tasks that need doing, there is also the need to interact and cultivate Facebook and Instagram profiles, all for the purpose of being envied by our peers and friends from school. The personalities that we need to assume multiply, and our thoughts dash hastily from deadlines to programs and obligations. We feel we're in a long Formula One race and that we're waiting for the weekend for a pitstop that will allow us to catch our breath. Yet the weekend is filled with more activities that tire us out rather than refresh us.

We must have the ability to correctly and adequately deal with pressure to perform the various roles that life requires us to play. For those with difficulties surrounding food, it can be a source of stress and ignite the search for culinary comfort: an illusory consolation that keeps us company in the stress of fulfilling the checklist.

An effective way to reduce stress and avoid becoming entirely overwhelmed by the tornado of performance anxiety is to break it all down into pieces. First of all, focus on the daylight hours of today; only make reference to a brief period of time. Do not look at the week, month or year, but only view the twelve hours that appear in front of you that morning.

Break the day into small segments and concentrate on each one, as if afterwards there is nothing that needs to be done. Living one event at a time is the key to not being swept up under the avalanche of emotions and worries that push you to isolate yourself from the world, searching for a happy oasis far from the difficulties through the comfort of food.

On a side note, if you want to be happy it is important to get your sleep. Almost all people need at least seven hours of sleep for at least four days a week. There have been many studies showing how sleep does increase wellbeing for more information check out: pursuit-of-happiness.org.

I recall the advice of American writer Joyce Meyer, in one of her speeches about the necessity of living in the present, to postpone all arguments concerning the resolution of problems and concerns to a specific day of the week, and to realise that when that fateful day arrives, more than half of those problems no longer present themselves as such.

Chapter 15
Start from Scratch,
with Excitement

All of the strategies suggested in these pages, created so as to transform one's life and obtain a balanced and healthy physique, require as their principal and determining factor – a certain spirit and emotional approach with which these concepts must be put into practice.

The enthusiasm with which you face your day is an essential component, without which you wouldn't be able to make the effective and lasting change in your life that will lead you to the achievement of a healthy and salubrious physique. Change is inevitable but it is also good.

During the most difficult periods in our lives, we often think that the best way to survive is to settle down and wait for the storm to pass, before getting back on the road again.

At the mercy of circumstances, you tell yourself: 'this too shall pass', 'life is made up of moments like these', 'the day will arrive when I feel better', 'the meek shall inherit the Earth'.

It's difficult in these circumstances to decide to intervene, despite the difficulties and gloomy skies, and take the helm of the ship of life, with enthusiasm and determination. But when it comes to living your life, nothing will get done unless you actually do something. Take the bull by the horns or that mental cricket by the wings and lead it to where you want to go. You are the boss of you.

I know that you've tried everything, and have rightly developed a level of scepticism towards anyone who would try to propose a formula of eternal happiness to you.

Regardless of what your life looks like today, you can step in and decide that it's not too late to roll up your sleeves and once again try to get excited about adopting a new lifestyle. Besides, what if we could find gratification in challenging ourselves to a path towards the expansion of our pleasure?

Chapter 16
Give Time to Time

Magazines and social media are filled with mesmerising advertisements for weight loss pills, fasting and starvation diets, the likes of which are designed to give consolation to millions of women who, after having survived some form of food autocracy, such as a diet, wander in search of a miracle that allows them to finally enter them size-zero paradise. (Now think about it, does size-zero make any actual sense? Air should be size-zero, nothing else.) In the face of the Goddess-making diet, the costs, sacrifices and physical suffering will always be a second-place consideration.

Then we have the depressing web, with its blogs on anorexia. These have endless advice on stomach sealing, the ingestion of dangerous chemicals and substances, and encourage frighteningly young women to experiment on their health, using extremely dangerous methods for the immediate loss of a few pounds.

Whenever I recount the extraordinary formula with which I finally succeeded in achieving a healthy lifestyle, after years of psychological and physical see-sawing, I get a single reaction. Worried, they ask me: 'But, how long did this all take?'

I'm willing to bet that, while reading these pages, your cricket has been muttering at you to try, once again, a 500-calorie diet, so as to lose weight in time for your cousin's wedding.

I'd like to remind your Jiminy Cricket that you've already followed hundreds of weight loss programs, and if you're still searching for the key that will free you from the bonds of physical discomfort, maybe it's time to broaden your horizons and see the possible existence of a long-term change, one that will help you escape the prison of dieting, and never look back.

'One month left until summer', 'Two until the school reunion', 'Three until that work dinner' and 'four left until Christmas'. Social events seem to occur in quick succession, uninterrupted, making us fantasise about entering the scene, beautiful and smiling, in a pastel-coloured body-con dress. Men will melt, women will wilt in envy.

I would invite you and your faithful yet annoying talking cricket to breathe deeply and to consider some simple logical reasoning: if it were your daughter with this problem, would you advise her to try the apple diet, lose a little weight, go to that party in shape, and to then, in the successive months, start the rollercoaster all over again with gorging caused by hunger, stress and nerves? Or, would you advise her to, once and for all, abandon any comforting thoughts promised by the phantom of dieting so that she can finally begin a wonderful new era of her life, characterised by balance, healthy food and the discovery of new passions? I have no doubt that you are an expert in the imparting of unbiased and sincere advice: perhaps you could consider the fact that there is, just like that theoretical daughter, a young you, just as much in need of this wisdom.

Following a method of balance, by nature, means you cannot have everything under control. You won't know the exact date of when you reach the finish line. Yet with a new consciousness and a new intellectual maturity, you'll be prepared to get rid of any thoughts of dieting. Those phantoms had you believe it was you in control, but in reality, it was they who controlled you.

Chapter 17
The Point of No Return

By focusing on the needle of the scale, you live in a state of self-induced trance, unaware of time, of events, and of the opportunities that pass before you. I would bet that if you evoke an occasion from the past, you would have no difficulty in recalling your physical condition or your outfit, but have a hard time remembering the conversation you had with a friend or relative. Don't worry, it's completely normal. Millions of women approach the scale with an attitude of awe, electing it as sovereign judge over that which we are permitted to do, say or think.

'If you can fit into that dress, then you may have fun, accept an invitation to dinner, or go shopping'. For years you've lived under a bell jar: the looming shadow of the scale-imposed deprivation and transmitted insecurity. If you think your ideal weight is X and that after having reached that you'll be able to live in the world of free women, you are lying to yourself. But don't worry, everybody does it without realising it. Only know that when you realise it, you can control it.

Think for a moment about the reasons for which you want to reach that weight. I can see you listing, off the top of your head, a series of motives that you've heard repeatedly on the television and radio: 'For issues with health, to be more active, be able to buy clothes in the big department stores'. But if you listen attentively, this desire to lose weight, to conform, to make yourself smaller is dictated by a desire to avoid comparison, to vanish in the eyes of others and to pass unseen by those Barbies of the gym who observe you while you do your aerobics. The first realisation you'll have, reading these words, will be: 'no, that's not true in my case. I have to lose weight because my doctor told me to'. Let's, for a moment, forget about the medical journals and consider honestly: wouldn't it be easier if you could pass unobserved in a standard size? Throw out the scale. The time to be realistic and to transform your life has arrived. Throw it out now, go, grab it and get rid of it. Maybe stomp on it a few times for good measure.

The moment of accepting that you aren't simply a number, is here, and distancing yourself from the scale carries with it the relieving liberty of no longer being categorised by a bar code. Follow this advice and together with the changes indicated in this book, you will finally achieve a healthy and balanced physique ... forever! The decision to say goodbye, forever, to the scales, diets and weight loss products signals a point of no return. You will never again want to go back. It is certainly inevitable that you'll experience small relapses: you've lived for years with the conviction that you were defective, you'll need time to really get your head around having lived in a *Truman show*.

A friend and colleague, excited about the advice to abandon any weight loss program and get to know herself by rewarding herself with healthy and delicious earth-grown foods, recently revealed that she was finally ready to buy a house, adopt a dog and marry her life partner. Determined and happy, she told me of the projects she was involved in and how she was experiencing a wonderful period of serenity and satisfaction. Since she had detached her mind from the obsession with food and the severe judgments of the scale, she was able to see more clearly, becoming aware of the marvellous dimension in which one can live once you have done away with every imposing structure related to the world of before and after. Good job you! Good job!

Chapter 18
The Wardrobe Detox

A fundamental detox for achieving a healthy and balanced body weight is that of the wardrobe. To start a purification of the body, we have to start with that of our mind, and what could be better than liberating the dusty, guilt-ridden rooms, full of drawers and boxes of clothes of all sizes, reserved for that magically more of "when you lose weight"?

Countless weight loss programs advise keeping in clear view the skirt that you could get into ten years ago, so that by focusing day by day, broccoli by broccoli, you can imagine the day that you're able to wear it. This is the same logic and methodology behind every weight loss diet and is doomed to fail. Ten years have passed and, fortunately, you've changed and matured. Suggesting that we worship, daily, a skimpy garment will only make us feel flawed and inadequate: as if participating in a marathon against time: always remaining behind, frantically panting while we try to reach first place while time taunts us. You are free to start the maple syrup diet if you want, and tired and frustrated, squeeze into that scrap of fabric. But we know that at the first emotional setback, you'll have to start all over again, defeated and humiliated. Aren't you tired of this predictable, destructive pattern?

Get rid of all the clothes that don't fit you anymore. You're about to start a real transformation: it's time to renew the environment that surrounds you. Don't keep war trophies, take everything and hand it over to a charity that collects clothing for the poor. Your house will be less cluttered and so will your mind.

Plus, you'll feel good about giving! Accept, with peace, that you are as you are: today, now, in this exact moment. You recognise and accept yourself for what you are. In giving this serenity to yourself, to your environment and to the food you ingest, you'll be able to get out of this infernal cricket balking cycle, that which is repeated periodically, as if, once wounded by the harpy of the weight loss diet, we want a return encounter, sadly hopeful that this time it will be more forgiving.

Having clothing that doesn't fit, is equal to judging our body and making it feel flawed, as does any kind of diet. In doing so, we would have not its collaboration for a new program of psycho-physical evolution, but its opposition and hatred. With time, as you improve your life through the advice of this book, and you reach a healthy and energetic physical form, you'll be able to go shopping and buy a new skirt, one that doesn't evoke a past period of your life and a representation of a you that no longer exists.

Chapter 19
It's Possible to Combine
Healthy Food and Friendships

Extreme and unsustainable weight loss programs have led you to the supposedly irrefutable confirmation: the equation diet + friends is equal to failure. The words "dinner" and "party" sow panic in your mind, making you a PhD in low-calorie cocktail combinations.

Trapped in a world of multiplication and addition, you admiringly observe the "normal people" who, carelessly enjoying the company of friends, won't have to suffer through the cricket's morning-after lecture on the imperative of a detoxifying fast.

For years, I have avoided events held by my friends, to avoid "losing control" and going overboard. How many social occasions have you relinquished, manipulated by self-destructive thoughts linked to your appearance? For all the joys you've deprived yourself of, have you found the formula of serenity in a healthy body?

I'd like to invite everyone, including myself, to reflect upon that future time, coming to the end of this incredible life experience, when we will look back sentimentally at the events of the past, and sadly we'll wish we'd had more strength to damn those limiting thoughts to hell, and enjoy that beautiful evening made of toasts and laughter. Humans are pact animals; we like to help people and be with people. Go out and find your pack, even if not human (time spent with my dog is the best time of my life).

Chapter 20
The Importance of
The Zen Hormone

To live in a serene, healthy and balanced body, it is essential to cultivate our happiness hormones. Picture yourself exhausted after a long day at work. Having just arrived home, your boss once again calls to ask a favour. Which carries a higher chance of your positive response: a kind request, or a command, shouted with agitation? The answer comes naturally: in order to collaborate with others, with ourselves and with our bodies, we need to abolish agitation and stress.

To help our body understand that it's finally over, that era in which we raged at it, abused it and forced it to commit to a starvation diet, we need to make it clear that from now on, calm and serenity have priority. An important way in which we can put this new paradigm into practice is to be aware of certain hormones that can be stimulated to induce a state of "Zen" within us. Serotonin is a neurotransmitter vital for our psycho-physical serenity. There are numerous foods that stimulate its production: banana, avocado, flaxseed, pumpkin seeds, poppy seeds, chia seeds, sesame, ginger, lentils, chickpeas, peas, beans, broad beans, miso, blueberries, spinach, asparagus and oats.

Discover the countless ways in which nature can make you smile and try to introduce these foods into your daily diet, whilst supporting your mood at the same time. The improvements in your physical state can only be a consequence of these changes.

Endorphins are another fundamental ally for our sacrosanct psychic peace. These calming hormones are produced when we move. We can start stimulating them with simple movement: walking in the park or pedalling or stretching while watching our favourite series. Nothing has to be frenetic or extreme, our body is very sensitive in this period of healing and needs to detoxify itself from the stresses of the past. Even standing up for a bit while you work can help. Magnesium in the evening can be quite helpful for deep sleep and a vegetable-based multi-vitamin in the morning to start your day can help you be more energetic and focused, having woken rested and refreshed.

It also appears to be true that some people are more genetically prone to happiness than others. But remember, even then happiness only seems to be about 40% genetic another 10% can be due to our current environment, events we can't control. The rest – the other 50% is under our control.

Chapter 21
Dinner in Northern Europe, Seasoning in Italy

In addition to the famed eight hours of sleep recommended for a healthy and glowing appearance, I strongly advise you to adopt the Northern European habit of eating early, very early. Having resided in Italy, Spain and Belgium, I've had the evening meal at seven, nine and eleven at night, and without a doubt, the time I've found to be the most adapted to a healthy physique was dining in the sunlight: the late afternoon is the ideal time to have our last main meal. To say goodbye to nightmares and heaviness of stomach, you and your family should get used to moving dinner forward in the day, it might be a good idea to eat when you return from work and then enjoy the rest of the evening freely, almost like having a second afternoon. It can be done be receding the hands of the clock by ten minutes per day. Introduce this fundamental change for a healthy and energetic body and you might find the effects quite surprising.

Interesting cultural side note: The people of Costa Rica (one of the happiest countries in the world) make lunch their big meal of the day. It makes a lot of sense to eat the most calories in the middle of the day when you still have many hours of work, play and calorie-burning in front of you.

Travelling around the world and living in an international environment, I've experimented with different culinary traditions and have noticed that certain cultures love to douse everything with sauces, from salads and sandwiches to vegetables. The food ends up submerged in condiments that alter their taste and nutritional properties. When you dress your food, imagine you are in Italy. Say yes to olive oil, vinegar, basil, oregano, parsley and onions.

The rest should be considered "strange". My mother always told the anecdote of an American uncle who had decided to surprise the family with a trip to Italy. Delighted to have him, my mother and her sisters busied themselves with complex and sophisticated menus. They had specially prepared a lunch comprising of sea bream and fish carpaccio, considered a prized meal in Italy. Sitting at the table, Uncle Franck looked at the abundance of elaborate dishes and without hesitation asked: 'Where's the ketchup?'

A preference for simpler foods also means getting used to simpler and more natural flavours. Experiment with the oils available at the nearest grocery store. Sesame, avocado, sunflower, olive and coconut oils are exquisite variations that you can easily use on your salads and raw dishes with surprising effects on your health and your body. A recurring nightmare situation in all low-calorie, weight loss diets is the loss of fats in the diet. For years it has been mistakenly blamed as responsible for the extra kilos and hence vilified. 'Just a teaspoon of virgin olive oil,' thundered the dietician. *It'd almost taste better if I skipped it completely,* I thought to myself.

Once again, it's clear that slimming programs do not reflect reality in regards to food and eating, that should be accompanied by healthy advice aiming to improve our bodies. On the contrary, they are sad programs that calculate and divide food into the good and the bad, deceiving desperate people only want to do what it takes to feel better.

In my consolidated experience, where I have succeeded, the key is to favour simple healthy foods from the earth (from olive oil to mayonnaise) and consume them following instinct and moderation; neither a teaspoon nor a glass, but a satisfying amount.

Chapter 22
Consult Your Body

For a healthy and energetic physique, it is essential to have an idea about which foods give us love and are in accordance with our body, and which don't enjoy an excellent relationship with our digestive system. Feeling bloated and uncomfortable is usually caused by the fact that some foods aren't compatible with our own organism. Sometimes we just have to accept this possibility and ask for help from a medical professional. Blood tests specifically for food intolerances could shed light on the situation. It could be something as simple as gluten intolerance. I am not suggesting that you start depriving yourself of food groups: that is not sustainable nor does it last long. Simply find out which foods are less than suitable for your physical well-being and keep them in mind. BTW, gluten intolerance is much more common than most people think and quite easy to deal with. One of my colleagues has a mate who is a doctor of Food Science. They note that many people may even mistake gluten allergy with lactose intolerance.

I am not a doctor so I cannot claim specialised knowledge on this topic, and yet, as a patient, I know full well that even the mention of a simple food sensitivity can, in the world of dietary emotions, trigger a relapse into the hell of restriction, diets and self-destructive mechanisms. Being aware that a food does not make you feel at your peak means accepting the idea of being able to try alternative foods, equally delicious and nutritious. Supermarket shelves abound with all kinds of food substitutes, and intolerances of lactose, gluten, eggs or wheat can easily be remedied with alternative products that sustain us and also give us pleasure. In this internet era, healthy and natural food solutions are well within reach for everyone. Products with ingredients derived from animal hooves, hormones and GM soy can improve your mood, your health and by consequence, your body.

Chapter 23
The Renunciation of Food

Many, many women are constantly on a diet, and having reached a healthy weight, have decided to forgo the pleasure of food. In order to maintain the results of the restrictive diet they had followed for years; they end up feeding themselves on air and some vegetables.

Countless studies demonstrate that low-calorie diets irreversibly slow down the metabolism, leading to always having to eat less in order to maintain the results obtained. Don't lose the pleasure of eating. Discover new, exciting recipes and culinary combinations. Put as many natural foods from the earth in your shopping cart and you will see that your body, allied with your brain, will take care of the rest. Our brains are much more powerful than we give them credit for. It's important to harness that power for good! If you eat one chocolate bar a day, your brain will send you signals that you'll perceive as "cravings" but that in reality are only reminders, triggered by repeated habit over time. Our minds love a routine. Take advantage and introduce delicious and wholesome foods into your day, and you'll find that your body and your mind will help you, requesting that you continue with this healthy habit day after day.

The media and publications persist in dispensing bankrupt notions that dictate nutritional formulas and spreading myths to those struggling with food. Thanks to this propaganda, some myths, in the public imagination, are irrefutable truths. One popular catchphrase is the importance of breakfast: 'The most important meal of the day'; 'Eat like a king'; 'Kickstart your metabolism'; 'Lose weight with breakfast'.

The theories about this meal are innumerable and they all incite us to consume a large and nutritious meal. When in fact Dr David Levitsky of Cornell University actually advocates skipping breakfast as a means of weight loss.

I have tested every weight loss diet on the market, met dozens and dozens of dieticians and nutritionists, I've had myself hypnotised, I've tried acupuncture and other over-the-counter methods and I can confirm that the only winning method, the one that led me to achieve a stable and natural existence is to listen to your body. Follow your instincts and forget about the rules: relating to diet, to breakfast or anything else. Read this book until you know its contents by heart, and you will obtain astounding results without restriction or neuroticism.

Chapter 24
A Day Off

The underlying basis for achieving a healthy and balanced physique is to not deny yourself anything. Long term deprivation brings frustration, rebellion and loss of control. People need to feel in control. A striking example of the perversion of mind, triggered by giving up one or more foods, is the disconcerting practice of the 'cheat day': a widespread practice encouraged by dieticians and nutritionists. I clearly remember the first time I heard this expression, and the feeling of confusion it elicited in me. In high school years, a friend once informed me about a miracle dietician: she managed to make her patients drastically and suddenly lose weight in an extremely short amount of time. Without even letting her finish, I had made an appointment and convinced my mother to accompany me, an hour from the city centre, to meet this weight loss guru. The diet that was prescribed to me consisted of foods weighed by the milligram, selected and analysed with fanatical precision. The list of foods prohibited was very long. What left me speechless is that the doctor then, after having essentially prescribed me steamed air to eat for the week, excitedly told me that on Saturday night I could eat whatever I wanted. Strangely, I couldn't make reason of the radical inconsistency between regime during the week followed by the authorised feasting. He continued, explaining to me how this method brought a shock to the metabolism, or something of the kind. As a patient and someone who discovered the formula that led me to achieve an effective and lasting psycho-physical balance, I can confirm that there is nothing more harmful, for those with difficulty surrounding food, of excesses. Deprivation and "cheat days" are the enemies of our physicality. Barely eating or stuffing yourself are failed mechanisms that will lead you towards a conflictual relationship with food and to the increase in your stress levels. This mechanism has a negative effect on how we feel and what we look like. If you want a chocolate bar, eat it. If you feel like going out to dinner with friends, do it: quietly and freely.

Don't focus on 'losing' weight, 'depriving yourself' of food, "giving up" on a dinner out. Think instead of the abundance available to you, with which you can revolutionise your life: "buy" health, "fill" your kitchen with healthy foods, "reward yourself" with deliciously nutritious foods. Let your new, healthy food choices sink into your mind, and your body will follow. Think positive things and positive things will happen.

Chapter 25
Prepare Your Mind for Success

Believe in yourself. You have so far failed to get the desired results not because you were wrong, or because you have no willpower, because you didn't have the time or because you like to eat. You simply didn't have any way to know what was the right method to obtain a healthy and energetic physical form. Today, thanks to this new knowledge, and to your abandonment of any sentence that brings together the words diet and stress, you have the tools to free your life of everything superfluous that for years has invaded your mind. Your new codeword will be "serenity". Whatever crosses your path, be it an event, person or food … ask yourself if it contributes positively to a state of calm and serenity.

You have the power to leave everything behind: suffering, failure and tears. They are part of a past, to which you may feel grateful because thanks to those difficulties, you have succeeded today in discovering new ideas that will bring a complete change to your life. Be kind to yourself, and imagine a reset of your experience to the moment when it all started. Go back to a time before this battle started and breathe deeply … you have another chance. Your mind is very powerful. Use this power to teach the cricket in your head to stress the positive and learn from and then ignore the negative. You can be what you want to be, you are the queen of the world!